Book of Prophecies

Cesar

authorHOUSE®

AuthorHouse™ UK Ltd.
500 Avebury Boulevard
Central Milton Keynes, MK9 2BE
www.authorhouse.co.uk
Phone: 08001974150

First published by AuthorHouse 11/16/2011

ISBN: 978-1-4678-9550-7 (sc)
ISBN: 978-1-4678-9551-4 (e)

Preface

Greetings to all who read this, especially to The Two who will follow...

If God created the planets and stars, then who can say that He didn't form them in a way that can reveal the future. Don't the rules of the Universe apply to all that happens in our world, doesn't the moon control the tide of our oceans; is it not the Sun that gives us light and life?

It is not considered a blessing to tell the future, even if it has been revealed through Divine inspiration, because it is not a blessing to see bad things or terrible things which are destined to happen. It is not a blessing but it is a gift. For a long time I ignored the gift, until it became clear that there is a reason why I should see these things, whether they are good or bad things that I see was never the point. I have come now to share with you these things that have been revealed to me.

Maybe the calling to a path has been influenced by many things in my life, my life which is not unlike yours. We witness people starving in one Country whilst empty fertile land in another Country lies untouched because of borders, borders which were originally created to define nations and hinder war. We also witness sick men, women and children going untreated simply due to finance, who are we to say no to people who suffer? We witness many people whose one goal in life is simply wealth, yet when they die they cannot take their wealth with them. For all these reasons and many more, I have come to pass a message and a warning to you, this is not how God wanted life for us to be, and our methods, if left unchanged, will call disaster upon us.

The rich and the greedy will seek to gain from the information contained within this book, but only the worthy will understand the true meanings, the ones that are worthy in the eyes of God. It is the underlying goodness that influences and purifies prophecy, for it is not for us to know the future, prophecy is meant as a warning and as knowledge and not as a tool for greed.

God reveals through images, and through Divine inspiration just like in the days of old, for thousands of years God has communicated to the chosen through dreams and visions just like the prophets of old, not that I myself claim at all to be a prophet or anything of such a grand title. Nor do I claim to be a 'chosen one', as anyone can reach out and listen to God if they are willing to hear what he has to say.

It is through the Baptism of Fire that the gift of prophecy is released, and because it is a very special gift bestowed by God, one does not need to fear reprisals from those who might seek to judge or torment, for these things are beyond their comprehension.

The knowledge to be a prophet does not come to everyone, it's a certain set of circumstances in a person's life that reveals knowledge to that person, where other people do not understand simply because they have not had the same circumstances in life. Not that I claim to be a prophet at all, but there is a natural way of things which is revealed by God to some. And it is right that this knowledge is restricted, because the dangers and profits to a person who can see the future need not to be mentioned, the impact of foretelling the future goes well beyond the message itself.

It is impossible for mankind to understand the never-ending complexities created in the Universe, it is impossible even for mankind to understand free will. It is this inability that prevents mankind from being able to see the future without help, it is only God who possesses knowledge of all things, and all things that will be.

This is why prophesy is far reaching, seeing as though it is not man alone, only man with Divine instruction, therefore I ask you, does not prophecy in itself prove that God exists? This is why prophecy brings with it believers and non-believers, as belief in God requires faith as does belief in prophecy.

Anyone who is experienced in knowledge of the spiritual world will tell you that there are three main ways in which a person can come to tell the future.

These are of course Divine inspiration, Astrology and lastly demonic sources. As my spiritual father was given the gift of prophecy, it was a combination of Divine inspiration and in-depth knowledge in Astrology that he foretold the future, and I would claim that prophecy would need at least two sources of influence.

However, it has become clear that it is not as simple as just three ways; a fourth way has been revealed. This fourth way is not something new, it is something that has always been there, all the way throughout history, and therefore I cannot pass judgement on whether any previous prophet has used this fourth way. Especially because prophets have not explained their methods, for that is not important, what is important is the message.

It is this fourth way which has been revealed to me, combined with Divine inspiration that has given me visions and dreams, so that I can communicate what will be, and write it onto paper for you to read, and to pass on the message to give hope and to give warning. I do however not claim to be anyone special. I am just a man.

It is maybe God that chose to reveal this fourth way, as knowledge of Astrology in today's society has much changed since the time of my spiritual father. The movement and understanding of the heavens has been taken over by Science in an attempt to explain the creation of our world without God. And in Religions, people who study the meanings of the stars in the hope of foretelling the future are almost considered to be outcasts. And so, in revealing to me the fourth way, it releases me from the use of Astrology, so that I will not be judged by Science or by Religion.

But I am no different a man to any other, I have my weaknesses and strengths and I am a sinner, sin that must be atoned for. But I do however see that God takes mankind on journeys of hardship to test our strengths and to change us from what we were into what we will be.

Therefore if hardships push a man into sin, should he blame God who created the hardships? No, free will is, free will. God's work is not just to pass judgement on us sinners, but also to understand, this understanding gives us the gift of forgiveness, when perhaps we do not deserve it.

Therefore as these dreams and visions come to me, I make records so that this book will be written, secrets revealed, others hidden within. The fourth way, unlike Astrology does not reveal exact dates, and therefore as I stay clear of Astrology for reasons I have mentioned, I will not reveal when these things will happen. It is better this way as *clear instructions with exact times will influence the very ability of the events happening*, therefore if you come to fully understand my writings, do not take the responsibility of that knowledge lightly.

To others who may also be given the gift of prophecy, especially The Two, do not ignore the gifts you have been assigned, you have been given a job to do, so nothing should stop you, therefore I wish to offer you a little guidance.

As I have mentioned already, leaving aside the Science of Astrology, there are still two other ways (ignoring demonic influence), both combined to lead to prophecy. The first being Divine inspiration of knowledge direct to your soul, which solidifies in the form of dreams and visions. Secondly, the fourth way of which I previously spoke is a true gift, one which reveals complexities of people and the world in a way that lets you fit them together like a jigsaw puzzle. However, now I speak directly to The Two who will follow, you will be guided by God to these writings and maybe as yet, you are unaware of each other, if that is so, you must endeavour to search until you find each other, you Two will possess power that I have not, not a new way of telling the future, but a new way of revealing the Truth to the world, I am just a man pointing ahead, you Two will be so much more.

And now as mankind reaches the half-way mark of things foretold by the Presbyter, huge changes are on their way. Therefore I have gathered thirteen chapters, each containing thirteen verses (with twin cryptic interpretations) of things that have been revealed in the hope to give guidance hope and warning to those who dare to read them.

Thanks be to God,

Cesar

Book Of Prophecies

By Cesar

Kindness,
Achieved,
Longing,
Inherent

Chapter One

(i)

The business of the States which are United,
Will be deemed most successful,
It will be stable for many years,
But be warned as poverty follows,
In the eagerness to overcome the problems,
An event will occur which will consume it's sons,
Only hard work to undo your errors,
Will bring any luck

Cryptic Script:

I see a crow flying over a field of ripe yellow corn, the crow continues till it reaches a field of strawberries, here it lands and starts to gobble down the strawberries as if it has not eaten in weeks, but it is spotted by the farmer who holds in his hand a gun, but instead of shooting, he looks on and smiles.

(ii)

The wealth and reputation of the
States which are United,
Will push to fulfill more ambitions,
But this will make everything worse,
Causing affliction,
Suffering and grief,
A once favourable public image
will be dragged down,
And the people you wished to please,
With profit and success in
business will see the truth,
Because a traumatic event,
Will show how much you owe

Cryptic Script:
I see the drain of a bath, water twirling in circles, a
woman with long black hair now dressed in a white
towel, she looks up and sees eyes staring at her
through the window, a man in a blue hat is on the fire
escape, she screams.

(iii)

Striving for health and riches and pride,
Will sacrifice the balance of the environment,
The search for prosperity
Will become so intense
That it will spew trouble,
Stories to the contrary will emerge,
Planned several years in advance,
With the aim of hiding the truth,
The truth of people getting sick,
People who have died
And the damage done to the world

Cryptic Script:

I see a crab walking on the beach, it is caught by a dog, and carried in the dog's mouth to the dog's master, he ignores it at first, but the crab tries to run so the master stands on it and pulls off the legs, eating them raw, he sits back on his chair.

(iv)

People, seeking to fill ambitions
Make choices in whom to follow,
Being too trusting in false ideals,
Because these ideals
Support their own wicked plans,
On one side,
Esteem will grow for fulfilling those plans
But on the other side
Undesirable people will blame
their poverty and illness
And even death on those same ideals

Cryptic Script:

I see a circle, a triangle, two more circles, and then a cube of glass, neon green, blue light shines from it, a drill appears at the bottom of the cube and drills into the ground, and water is sucked into the hole that it makes.

(v)
A warning against your enemies
And their underhand methods
For they hate
Your expensive enjoyments
Whilst they suffer,
They will work hard
To threaten your neighbour
They wish to steal the land,
Goods and character and they will succeed

Cryptic Script:
I see a rabbit, it is too fat to fit in the hole so it gets stuck, a butterfly lands on it and helps to push it in, the rabbit runs, chased by fire, then by water, until an explosion kills it, blood everywhere.

(vi)

Once your neighbour
Has been overcome
You will chose peace over war
You will want happiness and esteem,
But trouble will grow,
You will have neglected it too long,
And will be attacked by sea,
And only people of honour
Will avoid destruction

Cryptic Script:

I see a flood consuming across the land, a flood of blue apples that consume the men, houses and anything in its path. Only the people on high ground survive.

(vii)
Change is ahead,
Death to men
Peril to ships
Those who seek rest will not find it,
For the Great River
Will rise higher than
Anyone ever expected

Cryptic Script:
I see an old bicycle leaning against a sign post with three signs on it, ataca 75, ros 64, ciab 98, a man wearing untied shoes takes the bike and starts to cycle, full moon shines down from above.

(viii)
People will only be able to watch,
And this cannot be defended,
Prosperity and success will cease,
The coldness of humanity
Revealed anew
And at the place ataca ros ciab
An uncontrolled reaction

Cryptic Script:
I see people kicking a football around a stadium, I
leave and walk outside, the stadium folds up and
disappears until a man on a bike goes past, then
the stadium reappears but it has a statue right in the
middle of it, made of worn rock, the statue is of a man
on a horse, he wears a helmet and carries a spear,
on the bottom a sign which reads 'Steve authorises
over tie ball'.

(ix)

A man, devoted but cruel
Who looks younger than he is,
Will have an affair
And father a child,
A trickster will attempt blackmail
And the man shall choose between
Judgement and the innocence of
His public affairs image,
His domination of the situation
Will only lead to a fall from grace

Cryptic Script:

I see a grey wolf, it hears a rabbit move, but the grey wolf runs in fear, two other wolves now chase the first, one is black, one is white until they have a face-off, an eagle dives and attacks the white wolf, the grey wolf runs and jumps and falls and keeps falling.

(x)
A woman full of energy
Will give others a negative impression,
But the woman is strong,
And detaches herself from all judgement,
But she fears she will not progress,
Only seeking happiness,
Her doubt and fears increase
Until she realises
The potential for change

Cryptic Script:
I see a ballerina with red hair, wearing black make-up, she is dancing, afterwards she gets a yellow taxi, but the driver is a werewolf, so she gets out and runs into a bar to escape, but the bar is full of werewolf's, she looks scared but then she turns into a werewolf too.

(xi)
You have not paid enough attention
To your business,
And so you have to change plans
To build a strong future,
But be warned,
Do this wrongly
And you will end up looking stupid,
And all good news will move further from you

Cryptic Script:
I see a pole cemented in the rocks on the sea shore, there is a lighthouse nearby coloured red white red white, at night the Watcher comes and stands on the rocks, often waves break over him but he holds onto the pole, looking out to sea until dawn breaks.

(xii)

You will place trust in someone
Who will let you down,
This will threaten your finances,
As they will be stripped to the bare bones
That someone will need to explain
Before you can accept the situation,
And that 'power corrupts',
Then you will be happy but not wealthy

Cryptic Script:

I see a man who is scuba-diving to a wreck under water, where he finds a skull, the skull and the man converse 'it is not what it seems' 'what is?' 'Life' 'but why' 'because this is not how it is meant to be, power corrupts' 'can I take you somewhere?' 'take me home', the man holds on tight and appears on a beach, the skull no longer speaks, so the man buries it in a grave, and uses two sticks to make a cross.

(xiii)

The support you received
Will lead to important events,
To your annoyance
You will be forced
Into a financial situation
Where you will try
To do the right thing,
But create many quarrels,
This journey will bring
Many stormy days and plenty of stress

Cryptic Script:

I see a man with a golf club, he swings and hits a can, he recoils in pain, his thumb is broken, the can rolls away unbroken.

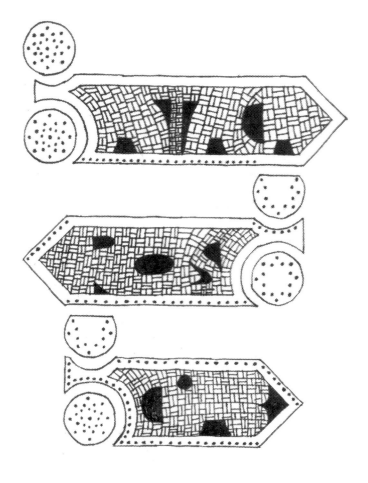

Chapter Two

(i)
It will become the ideal
To have faith
In a child's wisdom,
Although good in theory,
It will lead to a discovery,
A son plots against a friend
And it will cause much pain,
A son, whose social interactions
Has led him to the impulsive act
Which he regrets

Cryptic Script:
I see a fish with large eyes and big teeth swimming
in the water, a young boy with a yellow straw hat is
sat near the water and is fishing. He catches the fish,
and takes it to his father, who congratulates the boy.
Later the man goes to the pub to gloat, claiming the
fish as his own.

(ii)
Unfruitful labours
Never lead to gain,
Grief caused by a domestic problem
Leads to a demotion,
Someone else is promoted in stead
But they have a loose tongue,
This brings
Judgement and quarrelling

Cryptic Script:
I see a tree, rich with bananas. Below a man starves for food but cannot climb up the tree. A monkey laughs at him and climbs the tree and starts to eat the bananas. The man throws a stone and kills the monkey and eats it instead of the bananas.

(iii)

Cut off your compassion
For your business,
It is in danger,
Invest your efforts elsewhere,
A child of destitution
Escapes a life of loss,
Inside burns strong commitment,
Strength and intuition,
You must help him,
Or else he will be deceived
And brought into Fire

Cryptic Script:

I look down upon reflection in the ice, and see a wonderful tree in red-brown leaf, it is stood in the moonlight, hundreds of birds, bats and all manner of flying creatures fly past this lonely tree. A single leaf breaks from the tree, falls, and breaks the ice that I am stood upon.

(iv)
A great mountain,
That demands respect
And wisdom to journey there,
An innocent person approaches it
More at risk to be hurt than others,
Becomes separated from the group,
They work hard to find the lost person,
But their friend may be dead

Cryptic Script:

I see a purple pram, the old-type of pram and it has white wheels. A woman rocks it gently, she is wearing a black veil and they are in a park by the water, ducks swim over wanting food, but she does not have any to offer to them, so they start to eat her black dress.

(v)

This person
Had promised themselves
To conquer the Great mountain,
And worked hard,
Before even setting out on the journey
Some will be grateful
That the others were spared,
Some will be in sorrow or denial
And some will say
That it was not right
For someone of that condition
To travel to such a place

Cryptic Script:

I see a turtle, its green, and it swims onto a beach, where it lays five eggs before returning to the sea, of the eggs, a snake takes one, a bird eats two others, and one is taken by man and the last by another turtle.

(vi)

O the grape-rich,
A lawsuit will
Be decided against you
For you have failed
In your ability to make a living
But also you need to solve
The fact that you have been defrauded
Conflicts will make you change perspective,
To grab independence
And make the changes that you need to.

Cryptic Script:

I see a squirrel on the bonnet of an abandoned red car, it is eating a nut, but another squirrel approaches wanting the same nut. The first squirrel places the nut on the edge of the bonnet and the two squirrels fight. A third squirrel sneaks up on them and steals the nut and hides down by the wheel of the car, the other two have not even noticed him, and they fight on until they fall through the window and release the car brake. The car rolls over the third squirrel.

(vii)

An unusual experience
Will bring advancement and success,
You have gambled upon
Several dangerous enterprises,
And now you face a speedy
Rise to a good position,
Three bad fortunes now broken and put behind
Sorrow, bad luck and an unfulfilled promise,
You have learnt the lessons of the soul.

Cryptic Script:

I see a Japanese man sat meditating on the floor of a Japanese house, there are two swords crossed and hung on the wall, and a cloth hangs with letters on it. The Japanese man puts an egg on top of a lizard, and then on top of a turtle and slice them all in two with one blow from a sword.

(viii)
To drained stations,
Ever will increase the need for new
Resources or beginnings,
Loss, fire, lawsuits
Bring danger to your door,
Resources drained further
By business losses,
Take care of correspondence

Cryptic Script:
I see a 10p coin, it is finely balanced upon the edge of a grate of a drain, and water rushes down the street and knocks it off balance. It falls and falls till it hits the dark water below, there, it sinks into the pool and hits the bottom, and moss grows over it.

(ix)

You have much wisdom
Of the fine Balance
Seek courage
To face the stress of the decision,
And trust your intuition,
Courage to commit
To renew old acquaintances,
If you grow
Easy-going with the decision,
It will only further your stress

Cryptic Script:

I see a single white daisy, standing in a field of green grass, a dog's paw comes down and squashes it and walks on. It is a brown bulldog out for a walk with its owner. The owner throws a Frisbee and the dog jumps and catches it but its paws once again land upon the daisy.

(x)

O slayer of the mighty trees,
The way you navigate situations
In life are reckless,
Forgetting wisdom for vigour,
Your situation will change,
Avoid travel,
Or your experience
Will be peace in death,
You are not on the right path

Cryptic Script:

I see a toy boat fighting against the current on a river, it's a white sailing boat with a red and white sail, it starts to go backwards so a young boy rescues it, and the boy is wearing a blue top and brown trousers. The boy takes the boat to his dad, who refuses to do anything.

(xi)

A good companion proves false
And takes from your happiness,
Now you must use all the energy
At your disposal
To find stability,
First independence
Then commitment,
Healing then attraction,
Then you will have
Financial and business success

Cryptic Script:

I see a fork sticking into a pile of hay within a horse stable, here there are stables for four horses, and each door has a coloured name tag, orange, brown, silver and blue. I feed the horses in order of the colours on the door.

(xii)
Strength of love
Brings a wedding,
But there is a downward turn
As the bride becomes sick,
Knowledge of negative
Brings difficulty,
Avoid risks and change your perspective,
You fail to express yourself
When surrounded by negative people,
Look to the innocent side of her,
Before troubles overtake you

Cryptic Script:
I see a red rose on the roof of a coffin. It is carried by six men who wear white suits and black ties; they carry the coffin up a hill and onto the edge of a cliff. A young girl in white approaches, so they unlock the coffin which holds the never-living and never-dying, and they put the girl in, and they close the lid, and they throw it from the cliff into the Sea.

(xiii)
You have inherited wealth
But it has sorrow attached,
A cunning thief wishes to marry you
And have family only for your wealth,
You need to remain calm
Through the flattery,
Great contention,
Time running out,
Chose the opposite

Cryptic Script:
I see a bunch of carrots, still with some soil on them as if they have just been plucked from the ground. They are in a wheelbarrow that is being pushed by a walking cat. An impatient person waits at a table, with a knife and fork in his hands, the person checks the time on their watch as they await food, eventually they are given the carrots but are unhappy at the sight of them.

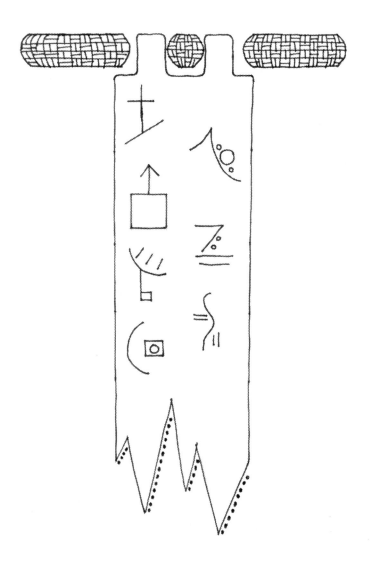

Chapter Three

A man of wholeness and harmony
Will have opportunity
For the limelight
But this will bring him beyond
His support network
And it will become a dangerous enterprise,
Have strength Jaril,
This is a life-marking-event,
Does happiness make you complete,
You need to be realistic
About your inner need
To control yourself
And everything around you

Cryptic Script:
I see a football sat on the penalty spot in a small pitch, there are goalposts with no net, behind a damaged wall has graffiti with writing on it, written in red. Above a twisted lamppost makes a creaking noise. A crowd gathers around and the ball levitates into the air to head height, I place it back down and kick it through the goal and it shatters the wall behind.

(ii)

A man runs from responsibility
And it will bring loss of affection,
Balance in your small ventures
May yet bring you freedom,
Quarrels over your neglect of responsibility
Will take you back to the beginning,
Things do not go well
With your wealth,
And your circumstances
May overcome you

Cryptic Script:

I see an ostrich running across the plains, on its back settles two ladybirds, one with two spots, one with three spots, from behind they are being chased by a cloud of dust, they arrive safe in the cover of a forest where the ostrich sets the ladybirds down on a leaf, the ostrich then hears one of its young calling from beyond but it cannot reach because of the dust cloud, so it lays down and curls up on the ground.

(iii)

A judged gossiper,
Off-balance and full of grief,
On the top of a man-made construction,
The gossiper perceives
To have been taken advantage of,
Unknown was the hidden danger
When the idea was sprung,
Will the situation
Overcome the emotions?

Cryptic Script:

I see a yellow frog sat upon a water-lily in the middle of a pond, up above an eagle soars and easily spots the yellow upon green and dives, but at the last moment a crocodile pops up and eats both the eagle and the frog, underneath the water, a nearby fish says 'stupid frog, doesn't he know that the yellow are the best?'.

(iv)

You must transform
How you live your life,
The simple life will succeed,
If only for a while,
Everything is overshadowed
By the Circle
Of Life

Cryptic Script:

I see a tree-log float down a river, someone builds it into a log-cabin, which burns down, the smoke rises and turns into clouds, which rain down onto the ground, and the water is soaked up into another tree, when that tree is cut down, the same thing happens again until all the trees are gone, the other plants now take the water instead, nature can only adapt so far.

(v)
A man that harbours bad feelings,
Self reflection
Has only shown him
How restricted he is,
His mind once peaceful,
Is now filled with chaos,
Chaos caused by a conflicted mind,
Control slips as offer is made
Leading to important event

Cryptic Script:

I see a man who works in a shipping port, his job is to tie the ropes to the pier, but the dark of the water always tempts him, he is John, one day he has a feeling about something bad that is about to happen, a ship looses control, and crashes into the pier splitting the cement all the way up to John's feet, then an anchor swings from the ship and hits him.

(vi)

A person with
An abundance of energy,
Who desires only to be loved,
At every obstacle
He throws his heart and soul at it,
Deceit in past,
Unease fills his mind,
Where will he find his pleasure

Cryptic Script:

I see a horse in a field, but it wants freedom. So it jumps a wooden fence to the next field which has high grass mixed with corn, the horse senses something, eyes watching, dangerous eyes, so it backs up. Then there is nothing but silence and the wind caressing the corn.

(vii)

Saving money is a perception of reality,
Self exploration interferes with your business,
So you ignore it
Until situations force you into such,
Is this being devious to yourself?
Things change for a second time,
A situation of great responsibility
Which will influence the future
Reality and wholeness

Cryptic Script:

I see a door with a window in it, a mouse runs along the corridor and cannot enter so it goes through a hole in the wall, a cat comes along and tries to enter the door and has to give up, a janitor tries to enter but can't, he returns with a ring of keys to try to unlock it, 47 keys in all.

(viii)
I see a strong
Old and established business
It has always attracted
Good investors
But the companies objectives
Become unobtainable
The company now three

Cryptic Script:
I see a red and white kite lying on the sand on a beach, it has a long string too, I pick it up and run till its in the sky, three sea-gulls land and I ask them what do they want, one answers 'to be loved' so I take them and build them a castle out of the sand from which they can live in.

(ix)

Do you have the wisdom
To overcome financial ruin?
Will you have your happiness
After trouble or will you
Push too hard?
Adapting has brought out your cold side,
An appearance of coldness grows,
Sorrow you have caused
Trying to balance the happiness
Of two opposing actions,
Respect now once actions explained
Take the necessary steps
On your path of evolution

Cryptic Script:

I see a white marble pillar in the clouds with a penguin stood on top, the clouds clear and I see the pillar sits upon a brain, then I realize its all a statue, a chisel breaks it into many pieces, an arrow points to a triangle beach where the broken pieces reform into a glass spiral staircase that's purple.

(x)
A woman in difficulty,
Devotion of her followers
Invade her personal space,
She lacks trust in honesty
And problems grow
With an ever growing need for freedom
She needs to do something
To make a muffled voice heard,
Before suffocation

Cryptic Script:
I see a grey car driving through the desert, it's an open-top-car and a woman is driving it, she wears sun-glasses and a red scarf which is waving in the wind, the scarf breaks free and floats into the air and it lands on a cactus, and gets stuck on thorns no matter how hard you pull, the sun goes down and the scarf freezes to ice.

(xi)

I see a man who keeps
At a distance from others,
Due to his difficulties
In life and refusal to reconcile
With those who done him wrong,
Important news will give him
A push on the road,
And he comes to realize
How weighed down he is
And he is negative and detached,
After re-thinking
He can overcome
Any barriers in his way

Cryptic Script:

I see a hamster sat on the arm of the sofa, behind a Christmas tree with flashing red lights in a spiral, below on the floor a toy truck, yellow and black is stopped at a stop-sign. Once the hamster is in the back of the truck, the stop sign turns to go.

(xii)

I see a solitude person,
A person of balance
Honour and beauty
Torn apart by a broken relationship,
This must be faced with bravery,
Take space and motivation,
Change vulnerability to balance,
Shine a light on the areas
Which prevent personal growth
And don't take other people's
Remarks to heart

Cryptic Script:

I see a lonely tree on a mountain, both covered in snow. Lonely trees get cut first. A man with an axe arrives and cuts it down and puts it on the roof of the car, and travels through streets with lampposts above, up in the mountain the stump mourns, the splinters mourn, an image, a ghost of a tree momentarily appears and then is gone.

(xiii)

I see a person
Who lacks appreciation of others
You are stable yet defensive,
But an unexpected visit
From relatives
Will force out the truth,
You are uncomfortable
And feel ashamed,
Take courage not to put
The situation on hold,
And remember
The passion within

Cryptic Script:

I see a chocolate bar on a kitchen top, it sprouts arms and legs, outside the sun is hot, the skin is starting to melt so the bar jumps down and attempts to open the fridge door but can't, so it lies in the shade. A grey haired dog comes along and eats it.

humble feet upon te
floor, fire lit in my roul
te crorr were he died,
te pat of my life,
rounor of creation,
te parrage of time,
open my mind to ty will

Chapter Four

(i)

Accept the end of the immature relationship,
All things require hard work,
For relations to work
Both sides must give faith,
Will and understanding,
Your innocence may be gone
But doubting your ability
To handle things is not
Being true to yourself,
First understand the past
Before seeking harmony,
There is no point
Pushing things deep into the mind
Which will only come back to haunt

Cryptic Script:

I see a brown teddy sat on the front seat of a pick-up-truck, the teddy is missing an eye, it belonged to a girl now dead, the father gets in, he kisses a picture of his daughter that hangs from the mirror and drives the truck through a wall and off a cliff, as he falls, he takes a deep breathe of air then he feels the cold water all around him.

(ii)

Go to the place of amusement,
Where people gossip of you,
An unusual dependency
Of being hurt and shattered hopes,
Give time for revitalisation
So that you know your resources,
So that your access energy
Can recognise the negative influences
In your life even if it means
The end of a relationship
So that you can start anew

Cryptic Script:

I see myself, I stick my head through a waterfall, behind is a Japanese woman with her baby, she is hiding, behind I hear noises of people looking for her and splashes in the water, I speak and warn her, she begs for time to say bye to her child so I make the water rush faster to slow the people down, she says her goodbyes and leaves to face her fate, I walk through and pick up the baby, a light shines from the baby.

(iii)
Dependence on ambition alone is unstable,
Ambitions don't offer
Protection against deceit,
Life is balance of good and bad,
If your achievements
Are not as good as you hope,
Will you lose control
And self-destruct?

Cryptic Script:
I see a mother and a boy-child playing on a slide, the boy is wearing a thick jacket, all around them is destruction, yet the two play on laughing and smiling, I try and talk to her but she shakes with fear of something we glance at the slide, now covered in blood.

(iv)

It will conflict with reality
And will cause chaos,
People may be in denial
But some won't be,
Those confused will seek comfort
To maintain a life of ease,
Lack of communication
Makes it worse

Cryptic Script:

I see a man working at an office desk, behind him is a big window of another office, its lights are off and the blinds are half closed. I look through and make out a dark figure rocking back and forth on a rocking chair, I go to talk to the man who is typing away on a typewriter, he types in-motion with the rocking chair, he turns and I see his eyes are black.

(v)
There is always difficulty
In keeping passion,
Relaxation, energy, and wisdom
Always helps,
But the real difficulty
Is maintaining life long love,
Which must consider
Attitudes and beliefs
And how one reacts
When life looses control

Cryptic Script:

I see a bonfire at night, it is surrounded by three tents, one blue, one red, one white, on the floor is a board with a half finished jigsaw. I finish it and it is a picture of three tall buildings and one small, then they are consumed by fire.

(vi)
Don't be too quick
To accept that proposal,
Your own perception
Has confused you,
It may solve big problems
But fuel problems at home,
Take time,
Important news approaches,
Control your wild side
So that you look no fool,
How you live is important,
Joy comes with news

Cryptic Script:
I see a front porch, there is a big window with patterned stripes, beyond is dark, day after day the postman comes and pushes letters through the letterbox for twelve days until the pile gets so big the postman looks through the letterbox and gets worried. The police are called and one talks to the neighbour while the other breaks in and sees the sitting room and a horror beyond belief.

(vii)

A huge transition approaches
That will create chaos,
Instability, corruption, indecision,
In attempt to deal with crisis
And increase happiness,
A lot of pressure
To resolve the issues
Will lead to rash decisions,
But indecision itself is rash,
Over-confidence in how
To deal with difficulty,
But fortunes decay,
Is learning from mistakes enough?

Cryptic Script:

I see a huge water balloon filled with milk or some other white liquid, it leans against a tree, a crowd gathers, 15, 25 and 32 and then it bursts and covers them in white, they are instantly sick and start to rot, so much so, that no-one can go near them and just drive past.

(viii)

The strength of an attitude
Is measured by its success,
Depth of experience
Helps to find answers,
Fear catches us in situations
That makes us feel alone,
But doesn't everyone suffer fear,
It will take hard work
To overcome your fears
But it is possible

Cryptic Script:

I see a man on the top of a building, he is wearing a hoody and looking down and watching the streets below, he is paranoid that a spider is crawling on his ear, the streets turn to water, spiders don't like water so he jumps and lands on cement, he gets up and his nose is broken, he looks at the people all around, and they all have a spider on them.

(ix)
Longing for strength of love,
Thinking and wisdom
Leads to awareness
Of the best part
Of humanity,
But find balance
As too much thinking
And examination will only lead
To a lack of excitement

Cryptic Script:

I see a red rose and a daisy growing but entangled together and fighting to grow the fastest. The rose is picked by someone for romance, the daisy by someone else as a friendship bracelet. These people, once the flowers start to wither, put the flowers in books to dry them out and keep them. One day these two people meet and the flowers are re-united.

(x)

A lack of protection against risk,
So don't loose your temper
If criticised,
There needs to be a
Change of structure of relationships,
And change to what a partner means,
But a risk in change,
You cannot stay divided
Between two beliefs,
Both sides cannot be happy,
Don't let pressure force you

Cryptic Script:

I see a cube cardboard box, sat beside a swimming pool, there is a lifeguard on duty and is sat in his high chair and sees the box so he climbs down, and looks at the white label on the box which has his name on it, he gets a scissors and opens the box. Inside is a silver bowl and as he lifts it out he sees in a reflection a body floating in the pool, so he panics and turns but there is no-one there, he slips and falls in the pool and becomes that body.

(xi)

Three seasons of bad fortune,
A reminder of the real world,
Two phases for the people
In your space,
Have compassion for visitors
Who have experienced much,
Many problems at same time,
Do not let discomfort bring out the cold

Cryptic Script:

I see three glass bottles of milk outside the front of
a house, the are sat in a metal basket, a woman in a
white dressing gown fetches them and brings them
in, she leaves one at a door, a second at another door
for her tenants, then takes the third to her kitchen
where she starts to warm up the milk in a saucepan.
She looks at me and turns to stone.

(xii)
A mysterious perspective
Builds in strength,
Born from within a place
Of negativity and judgement,
But it moves to areas anew,
New friends found,
Achievements abroad complete,
Now sanctuary needed

Cryptic Script:
I see a woman with blonde hair, beautiful and long,
she wears a red dress and walks through a black-tie-
party but is unseen, I ask why, she is a ghost, I ask
her why she haunts here and I take her to an oasis
in the desert where she can have peace.

(xiii)

A new experience
Is ready and revealed,
Frustration at an end,
Getting rid of habits,
New life given and great change,
Potential unleashed
But the bad held back,
Bad luck for old age.

Cryptic Script:

I see a boy cower in the corner of a room, all around there is shaking like an earthquake, sounds of glass breaking, I see a girl shaken off a tree branch, I see the earth open up and swallow things whole, and I see a person turn their back on the forsaken.

Chapter Five

(i)

Deceit about social pleasures,
Will cause situation tricky,
Loss of control,
Take care of the balance
If stubbornness changes plans,
Commitment to security
Make them restricted,
You must fear
The future potential

Cryptic Script:

I see a hole in a wrinkled tree so I look inside and it is hollow, I notice that from one branch hangs two ropes once connected to a swing, but one rope has broke, a small brown-haired doll in a dress lies on the grass, I pick it up, and from underneath a tree grows from a seed.

(ii)

A passage of time approaches
With potential for chaos,
We are in transition
Between stages of how
We connect to the world,
A threat could push us
To the past rather than forward,
Be wise at what you may loose,
You may avoid domination

Cryptic Script:

I see a grand-father-clock upside-down in a hallway, its hands are going backwards on its white face, then one after another they stop moving and point to eight o'clock, then the clock vanishes as if it had never been there.

(iii)

The innocence surprised,
A time of mourning
To the ones not fortunate,
Ideals born to resolve conflict,
Communication helps success,
Surprise of success,
Great honour in achieving the unattainable

Cryptic Script:

I see a white lady that roams the graveyard, she is all forgotten, but finds peace when she looks at the stars above, on her finger is a diamond ring, I ask what she wants and she says she wants to be a star, so I tell her to let her ring take her there, she holds onto it and is taken into the sky, where a new star appears in the sky.

(iv)

Success to perceive deceit,
Intense emotions of fear,
Fear of choice between two,
Wisdom of destruction,
The coming of war, fire and danger
Forcing the choice,
Undesirable man of great power
Takes away control

Cryptic Script:

I see the top of a hill covered in grass, burnt into the grass is the edge of a triangle and at each corner burns a white fire, down from the sky falls a ball of fire and it consumes the middle of the triangle, a hole made by the impact, a hand appears and a man crawls out.

(v)
You will realise the change,
Something sinister,
A strong and important person
Who is wise yet angry
Anger at Oregon,
Diligent unity
But better to be humble,
Loss, isolation and pessimism

Cryptic Script:
I see a cross or maybe an X, it changes shape to that of a man with outstretched arms, then it changes into the head of a red bull with pure white horns, the horns point to Oregon, circles spin and the circles twirl etching into the ground, all that is left is cold, barren and empty.

(vi)
Failure of efforts
To stabilise the chaos
When stability greatly needed,
A person powerful
Takes his chance
To oppress through power,
Jobs lost, control lost,
Many inhibited,
Many wish for the bad news to go

Cryptic Script:
Like the legs of a spider the water invades the land, a volcano explodes and burns my hand, lava flows and silences all, below a hairbrush sinks into the water.

(vii)
Our foundation is love,
But we grow cold and rigid,
Powerless to avoid danger,
Powerless to protect,
Energy to control poverty,
But sorrow comes,
Decay of health,
People separated,
Justice gone

Cryptic Script:
I stand with feet in warm sand, all I can see is ice approaching from all around, animals and insects flee, I have a sword with a beautifully carved handle, and as I hold it, it rusts and crumbles until it is no more.

(viii)
A complete observation
Of a changing stage brings humility,
Judgement over settlement of quarrels,
End of dangerous enterprises,
Settlement yet blighted hopes,
Joy that secrets are kept
Without need for answer
Until news from abroad

Cryptic Script:
I see a marble rolling along the floor of a long hall, a priest in black clothing chases it, the marble stops as it hits the wall at the end of the hall, the priest hides it in his pocket and walks to the garden, where he examines it, then he is struck by lightening.

(ix)

Protect your hopes and possibilities,
Protect the exclusion from luxury,
Trouble danger losses and peril,
As chaos moves across a Country,
The neglected achieve goals,
Indecision about sickness
Requires extra effort

Cryptic Script:

I see a hat in a window display of a shop, they sell umbrellas too, it is raining yet no one comes to buy them, a flood sweeps the streets so I climb onto the roof, houses destroyed, in the valley between the two hills.

(x)
An idea forms
To go from difficulty to comfort,
A transition
On how we see ourselves,
Too much energy too quickly
To try to succeed
Brings disappointment
And pessimism

Cryptic Script:

I see many trees on a mountain with snow on top, it reflects into a lake where I sit on a boat, a shockwave ripples across the water; the lake dries up and becomes barren where nothing lives.

(xi)

It is good to have
A strong peaceful existence,
Esteemed heights of experience
Can bring new beginning,
But lack of fear
At the eleventh hour
From the over-confident
And stubborn brings indecision

Cryptic Script:

I see a sea which is red, and I lie floating on the sea looking up at the night sky as the moon reaches eleven, three stars appear, one ahead of the other two.

(xii)
The truth of a phase of sickness
Not fully revealed,
Much anxiety and isolation,
Enthusiasm of protection lost,
Comfort threatened,
It is important to put strength
To motivation before opportunity lost,
Inadequacy, difficulty of strength,
Lost is the ability to bounce back

Cryptic Script:
I see a skeleton in an empty grave, half uncovered,
the empty eyes search the tall trees above, nearby a
red car pulls away, a large man with guilty pleasures
leaves nothing but tracks by tyre.

(xiii)
A favour asked by someone in need,
A person who can be helped,
Increased ability to appreciate the past,
But six disagree,
Six now wish your ruin,
Relax in safety of protection,
You will succeed

Cryptic Script:
I see a doll hanging from a piece of wood, below six worms gather to wait for it, but a cocoon forms around it and out bursts wings blue and green and it flies away.

Chapter Six

(i)

Thirst for elimination increase,
Envy of others in another Country
But courage needed,
Responsibility and judgement
From the world will come
So don't be careless
Keep your thirst closed in,
You need strength for responsibility,
Consider what you would do,
All your ideas,
And you will suspect the situation
May run out of control,
Reject the ideas
And keep to your freedom

Cryptic Script:

I see a kidney lying on a paving slab in a street, a dog picks it up and carries it and drops it into a yellow box and closes the lid, a man picks it up and places it on the back of his truck, opens it and sees a round fleshy cone, he closes the lid, leaves the box on the street and drives away.

(ii)
Wealthy with potential for growth,
Is humble despite success,
Triumphs over enemies,
Success but was on the brink,
Stubbornness helped them through,
Harmony with domestic issues
Freedom, yet out of control,
Consider how stable you are,
Clumsiness will make breaking point

Cryptic Script:
I see a golden vase on a marble floor, a ball lands and chips the edge of the vase, a second ball lands inside of it, a third misses and instead rolls around the base of the vase, then a forth comes and shatters the vase.

(iii)
A situation left ignored,
Indecision because of your anxiety,
Seek shelter in sanctuary,
Not ready to face the knowledge,
Deal with your small doubts,
Contented but be careful,
Risk of control,
Risk of loss of profit

Cryptic Script:

I see a creature sat waiting on the roof of a church, it is almost invisible yet horrible, it waits till Paul S comes out, then it follows him home, it is evil and will make him do evil things, things against his good character.

(iv)

You have taken things too easily
With the flow of life
Even intuition tells you
Harmony is not right,
You can feel that injury is nearby
From which you need protection,
Rise above the situation for success,
Stability needed against this danger
Else you will fail,
At the end you may overcome
And have renewed prosperity

Cryptic Script:

I see a woman in green floating on water, she turns into a jellyfish and then into an umbrella, which is picked up by someone on a boat heading to the land of hope, it is raining, once arrived the umbrella is thrown back to the water to be used again.

(v)

Strength to achieve comfort
Has now made you idle,
You commit to understand yourself
But not life itself,
Beware of approaching loss
And sever difficulties,
Being threatened,
Save as much as possible,
Remember the promise from your past

Cryptic Script:

I am at a bar in a small pub, I am sat on a bar stool, nearby is a man with a rotten face and he is wearing brown sackcloth, the barman comes and I order a whisky for me and the other guy, he thanks me and leaves, a wolf enters the door looking for that man and then leaves, then I notice that the man has left a ring, I pick it up and on it is engraved 'there is belief'.

(vi)

An overwhelming force
Of ill-luck by enemy unknown,
Their approaching goal, surrender,
You have the success,
To which they hope to destroy,
They will have joy
At your disunion and quarrelling,
Delay to the conclusion,
Their ways will make you fear,
And challenge you that
You will prejudice your enemy

Cryptic Script:

I see a giant centipede on my arm, it crawls along and then onto a leaf of a banana plant, all around are trees that are being eaten by loads of centipedes, they go from field to field, people scared of them, until the centipedes reach the sea and can go no further so they die and are eaten by birds.

(vii)

A person with domestic troubles
Will take a short journey
To meet a stranger,
Stability overcome by passion,
Be aware of an atmosphere of annoyance,
Information changes ideas,
Changes the sense of direction,
A long but not fatal illness,
Negative about being deceived but strong

Cryptic Script:

I am in a cabin on a sailing boat, on the table is a map of Central America but where there was one land there is now a sea, I go onto the deck, we pass some rocks on the new trade route, arrows fired, scared away by cannon, I look down and see an image of a snake ready to bite, it is red and black.

(viii)

In a free, overconfident world,
Warning of danger considered deceit,
Realisation of trouble
Due to your own misconduct,
Freedom but freedom of immorality,
You think you are happy
When you are actually vulnerable,
You have freedom to be cleansed
If you so choose,
A warning of danger
Unless you live well

Cryptic Script:

I see a three-leaf-clover in a field of green grass, above the cloud transforms into the shape of a clover, a cross with a loop appears and on it, it says 'here lieth Dave' and below three pink roses are in a jar filled with water, the cloud turns into an angel.

(ix)

Intuitions of practical solutions,
Your wish will be granted,
The unattainable of practical
With spiritual combined,
Great knowledge and creativity granted,
Be honest with your desire,
Do not be over-sensitive,
Do not worry about your situation,
Your fate is protected from evil,
Lasting joys for your future

Cryptic Script:

I see a woman descend the steps of a castle tower with a candle in her hand, she wears a red and purple dress, a secret way into a room with a four poster bed, where she undresses and waits but no-one comes, in the morning much sorrow and sadness on her face.

(x)
Accept success,
Erosion of promises
Wished to be fulfilled,
Death of a relation
Before hard task concluded,
Hard battle to explain
Actions to a friend,
Commitment and affection to a strong woman,
Desires sheltered from reality,
News of success
Comes from a distant place

Cryptic Script:
I am on the front of a boat travelling across water full of turtles and dolphins, we reach the beach and I get off, there is a strong wind all around me, I walk into the sand dunes and see a woman with brown hair that is blowing in the wind, she has a guard-dog, its bark shoots out lightning and thunder.

(xi)
Indecision about taking responsibility
Of how we lived our lives,
Anger and fear,
Potential hindered,
Gloom danger peril,
Protection overcome,
Place trust in someone
Who will let you down
Renewal drowned

Cryptic Script:
I am sat by a stream of water, I let my feet dip and the water is warm, I lay back onto the grass and look up at the sky which begins to cover with dark grey clouds and then it rains until I am soaked, I dive into the stream and under the water my clothes are now dry.

(xii)

Wisdom and experience will give
Assistance in great difficulty,
Wisdom of creative strength,
Wisdom of situations
Gone on too long,
Unselfish resolve,
Obstacle to overcome
To achieve our goal,
But difficulties more we face

Cryptic Script:

I see an old man with a walking stick, it has his
life story carved upon it, his hair is white and long,
people follow, 21 in all, and he leads to a mountain
and gets to the top as a storm approaches.

(xiii)
Protect the honest,
Good times will come,
Do not reject open opportunity,
Be warned,
A passage of time approaches,
Self destructive qualities
Will bring inappropriate actions
From within the community,
You need luck

Cryptic Script:

I see a coat with four medals on the back of a chair by a square table, I look at a calendar on the wall and see August the 27th marked, I touch it and see a river of blood running towards the feet of a man with an evil smile.

Chapter Seven

(i)
Do not contain fortune
Within barriers
Because of worry of the future,
Free, calm and methodical
But having to explain actions,
Undecided, regress or growth,
Many aspirations,
Regression chosen as the way forward,
Situations examined,
Growth gone,
Regression here

Cryptic Script:
I see a segment of an orange that has been left in a glass bowl on a picnic table on a beach, surrounded by palm trees, a boy and a monkey sit at the table, both stare at the orange, the monkey points with it's hand and the boy looks, the monkey takes the orange.

(ii)
Hidden truth of your pleasures,
All hope in attraction
What is your influence and power?
Explore your motivation,
Balance lost when attacked
By enemy unknown,
A bold negative statement,
Fear of how others feel about you,
Future danger sickness and sadness

Cryptic Script:
I see a sweet-wrapper, purple and silver in colour, it is opened and inside is a green lizard with a black stripe, everyone who touches it dies, and when it swims through the water, the water becomes poison to anyone who may drink it.

(iii)
A world of life
To be made easy,
Trouble approaches,
You will suffer great distress
For a short time,
Lack of enthusiasm for the future,
Wisdom to achieve will help you
Past the difficult situation,
The person with knowledge
Seeks to be heard,
Scandal and judgement of words,
Ambitions rejected

Cryptic Script:
I see a battleship by a harbour, abandoned, plates left overturned, it is empty, a white helicopter lands, people in white protective suits get out, their suits have black stains upon them, they have come to find the Cause, silence on the ship, the helicopter never leaves.

(iv)

Peace lost,
Change of awareness,
Follow your instinct,
Danger if you do not learn to cope without,
Thrown into a difficult situation
To see if you succeed,
Loss of two close friends
Makes you feel like you have failed
Listen to counsel

Cryptic Script:

The letter A, black fills the sea, birds and fishes die, at a place most precious, ship lost, danger, death, balance lost, sink with two, mistake, shame, problem unresolved.

(v)

Too much creation or rigidity,
Confusion in your life,
Be aware of what holds you back,
Confusion of feelings
When two return from abroad,
Humbled and undecided,
Situation examined,
Invitation for history to repeat itself,
Opportunity to amend old wrong

Cryptic Script:

I hold a carved wooden figure that I found by a bonfire, there is no-one around, I can feel the warmth, two trunks lie on the ground surrounding the fire, I sit and stare into the fire, I see faces, faces from the past, ones lost, times forgotten, then I see myself in the future.

(vi)

Strong wise cultures,
Culture upon energy and freedom,
Plan failed due to false friend,
A friend that you were once you devoted to,
But now disloyal,
Try to escape
Responsibility for the deceit,
Danger to your old friend,
Attempt to overcome accusations
To renew dignity,
Gift to be offered

Cryptic Script:

I see an Native-American with a white face and a design in red upon his forehead, he rides a horse, a grey wolf his best friend, upon his tent he paints his visions, but one day, whilst hunting a deer, the fabric around his tent is stolen, secrets gone.

(vii)
Great changes to Gas,
You desire to travel but you cannot,
Made humble,
Energy needed to change beliefs,
Recognised aggression,
Surrender to loss and adapt,
Contact with shunned
Provides solutions

Cryptic Script:
I see a pond frozen over with ice, I kneel onto the ice and wipe it clean, I see my own reflection, I punch the ice, making a hole, and fall into the cold water, the hole in the ice re-freezes over, and I see someone walk across the ice and look down at me, but that person is me, I curl-up.

(viii)
Responsibilities to maintain faith,
And confidence to move on,
Strength and success
Snatched from your grasp,
The wisdom of ANC,
Freedom from your negativity sought,
Fear of being overcome
By trickery,
You have outlived
Your usefulness

Cryptic Script:
I see a metal door on the ground, red and rusted with worn letters in white, but the door is attached to a buried car, so I open the door and a large green snake comes out and slithers away, inside I see an old snake skin.

(ix)

The indestructible Web,
Crossing a stage of life
To the artificial,
Wisdom of detachment
Of how we learn about others,
Learning judged,
Authority challenged,
Death and damage to wealth,
Resentment awakened,
Strengthened authority,
Indestructible weakened

Cryptic Script:

I see a stone bridge above a river of purple plastic, a man comes with a big mallet, he wears a yellow hat and his face is black, he hits the bridge with the mallet and the stone breaks and falls away, underneath is another bridge of silver and gold, he lights a fire upon it until it melts away.

(x)
Five integrated adventures
To The Core,
Repulsive challenge confronted,
Watch your health on your journey,
Two loose energy
And are in serious danger,
Three brave, three free and strong,
Fear of wasted efforts
But position assessed
Escape chosen

Cryptic Script:
I see five dead rats on the path of a street, two work horses pull a cart with three dead men in it, I open the sewer drain cover and climb down into the sewer, where many refugees huddle together, women and children.

(xi)

A Bomb in a place
Strong in business,
Concentrate to commit
To a plan to protect,
Bad domestic troubles change perception
And observation of the bad,
Fear of the unknown,
Fear of deceit,
Temporary escape gone
Self destruction on 12th street

Cryptic Script:

A kite flies, held by a man with long brown hair and
a black jacket, he hands the kite to a girl, her eyes
now black, she walks from the park onto 12th street,
the grass behind gone black, she passes a big old
grey building.

(vii)

Unsuccessful to borrow money
After a discovery of pain,
Great Angle changed,
Difficulty in understanding,
Narrow escape but violence follows,
Need to return to innocence
When you hear of death,
Dignity before anger,
Responsibilities and troubles
Blight hope,
Bad news,
Protection lost

Cryptic Script:

I see an Eskimo fishing into a hole on a frozen lake, he catches and lands a shark, he cuts open the belly of the shark and out comes a child who runs and transforms into a tiger, and the Eskimo shoots a gun and hits the tiger in the shoulder, the tiger hides in a snowy forest.

(viii)

Mystery unravelled,
The Great Eye,
In the year of 23,
Solution to a problem,
Speculation unfavourable,
Success needed,
Greater effort required,
Seek guidance from CONRE,
His help will make you avert danger

Cryptic Script:

I see a ferret upon a tree stump; it swims out into the river, dives and catches a fish, climbs out and runs to its young, passing a sign partially covered.

Chapter Eight

(i)

Person of worth, jumper from a plane,
Broken from domestic troubles,
Perception altered of hunger for life,
Loss to advancement,
Loss to worries,
Over judgemental examination,
Life energy deceived,
Happiness sold short

Cryptic Script:

I see a broken sausage on a plate being carried by a waiter up 122 steps, at the top the waiter goes through doors and into a large art gallery, an art critic is sat on a bench and staring at a painting, a painting of just red and orange colours, he takes the sausage eating one half and then the other.

(ii)

Near goats on a hill,
Prosperity meets days of storm,
Awareness of danger,
Grief through anger,
Don't blame others if not alert,
Wishing to return to profit,
You face much anger and many arguments,
Someone near do not trust,
Problem before harmony

Cryptic Script:

I see a hen at dawn waking the farmer, who fires a warning shot from a shotgun before returning to sleep, the hen returns to the nest where eggs number three and four, a fox arrives at the hen cage.

(iii)
Creatures of pool man-made,
Be careful not to be too quick
To accept a proposal,
Intuitions of peril,
Intuition root cause,
Sense the disguised imperfections,
If you worry,
Then seek to reveal hidden aspects,
Uncover scandal
But seek protection before chasing goals

Cryptic Script:
I see a rocking chair on a porch, I see a tree with
empty branches blowing in the wind, I see a woman
hanging clothes on a clothes-line, I see a bike falling
down to the ground, I see a tile loosen from a roof
and fall to the ground.

(iv)

Twin peaks of The West,
Judgers of the carefree,
An unpleasant situation approaches,
Strong communication of intolerance
Your foundation,
Content with steady progress,
Difficulty will soon surmount
Because of your own efforts,
Dignity taken,
Degradation of goals

Cryptic Script:

I see a yellow crayon dissolve into a puddle on a street, a man steps into the puddle with one foot and walks home leaving a trail of yellow footprints, a cat also walks through the puddle and climbs a nearby gutter onto the roof of a building leaving yellow footprints too.

(v)
Girl snatched,
Taken by man
Who feels hard-done-by
A man with little public
Position wealth or dignity,
Narrow escape from his urges,
Emotionless he escapes responsibilities

Cryptic Script:
A shed in a garden, secret hatch, do not let another in a ditch, find here the evil wooden cottage near 23 mile from Peterborough.

(vi)

Waves upon Palms,
Sheer wild beauty and raw power,
Life and commerce threatened,
Where is wealth when life passes to dust?
The caring show devotion
But something not smooth
With link to finance,
Soon need assistance,
It will be offered,
But beware, deceit

Cryptic Script:

I see a black cougar upon red background, emblem upon limo, pulled up at a movie premiere, a lady with silver hair and a silver dress gets out of the limo but trips on the red carpet, no-one helps her, they all just take photos.

(vii)

Discord above the Clouds,
Guidance needed to overcome,
Seek knowledge of old,
You can have lasting success
With lots of effort,
Understanding out of touch with the wisdom,
Think outside the box,
End to a way of life

Cryptic Script:

I see a radio operator on an old plane, Victor Charlie 203, he jumps from the plane and becomes a large white bird, below a small island surrounded by another shore, the letter R burnt into his mind.

(viii)

The Ramp shall yield,
Information of whom responsible,
Hesitance at unleashed scandal,
Overcoming guilt by threat to drag with,
Anger against the enemy,
Guard your tongue,
Observe in silence
Bide your time

Cryptic Script:

I see a sock and a scroll, I climb into the sock with the scroll and open it, it reads 'in time judgement' and then a list of names and crimes upon it, I roll it back up and climb out, a soldier knocks me to the ground and takes the scroll and opens it, his eyes are burnt out of the sockets.

(ix)

Time comes to explore
The repressed knowledge,
Fearing judgement for actions
You will seek to safely explore
Within a protected environment,
Sadness to face the past,
Too much responsibility lacking,
Your weakness has and will be
Your ambition to hold back words of truth,
Fearing reactions of others,
Making decisions for them

Cryptic Script:

I see a diver in a black wet suit on the coral reef, he swims past fishes and into the deep, the time left on his clock 22 minutes, attracted by a giant urchin, circle with square, it takes his arm off and then swallows him whole.

(x)

Through a passage of time,
The Web shall speed up,
Fear of disconnection from reality,
Steady from progress to anxiety,
Something you cannot understand yet,
Transition to another state
To lose bitterness and habits,
But what is given up
Is too important,
You must fight the difficulties of temptation

Cryptic Script:

I see a rattlesnake coiled, it strikes my leg, I fall to the ground in pain, an aborigine walks up to me and he says a prayer in another language and then moves on. I can feel my leg burn with pain from the poison, until I can take no more and surrender to fate, then I see tattoos appear over my arms, and I can feel the strength return.

(xi)

The scandal of The Barrier,
Speaking to an old friend
Gives you reason to weep,
Seek advice of the three issues,
Reconsider death by justice,
Your omen of success,
Bravery, work hard at this

Cryptic Script:

I see a stain-glass-window, below it a large choir sing, a third of the choir are robed in white, a third in black and a third in red, at the centre of the room is the person instructing the choir, lightning strikes all around him yet it does not harm him, he has horns upon his head, around him the floor melts and becomes lava in the shape of three.

(xii)
The Bridge from a high hill,
Power unleashed,
Loss on its way,
Methodical examination leads to a surprise,
Hard work to amend,
Serious set-back and chaos,
Sudden awakening,
Loss of control

Cryptic Script:

I open a door into a huge library, hundreds and hundreds of books all around, sat at a table a woman of purity dressed in blue rests her head upon an open book and sobs, I take the book and see a picture in it of an anchor at the bottom of the sea, I pick out another book from the many shelves but it shocks me.

(xiii)
Red horizon by huts of straw,
Anxiety against progress,
Forced to move for safety,
People unwilling to listen
Or understand their problems,
Communication the path to success,
Time to act but not on impulse,
Misfortune if you do not listen,
Do not trust acquaintances
Till time proves that they are true

Cryptic Script:
I see a skeleton raise up and walk a street, no-one lets it in, no-one hears what it says, it steps onto the road and is hit by a van shattering the skeleton and the bones go everywhere, then each separated bone becomes a skeleton that tries to speak, and they keep multiplying until someone has to listen.

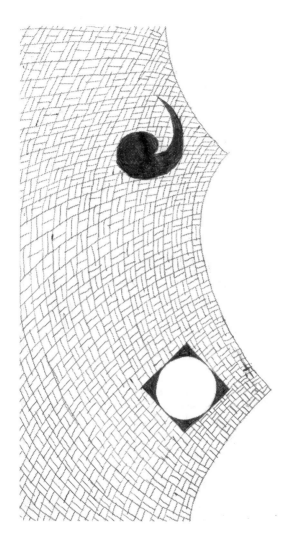

Chapter Nine

(i)

You don't need to lack excitement,
But you do need to have stability
In how you live your life,
Steady progress in life
Without fear of hopes not being fulfilled,
Do what needs to be done,
Be humble not to let emotions rule you,
Now take time
To replenish your energy
As troubled times are ahead

Cryptic Script:

I see grey dark stones lying on a dry river bed, there is no water, I walk upstream, dead trees cover the embankment, I find a waterfall, water falling from very high but it is taken into the ground before it can flow as a river, I take a cup and fill it but the water is gone before I can drink it.

(ii)
Reversal of fortunes of defence,
Prosperous ambitions,
With a further hidden dangerous ambition,
Destruction to your short lived success,
Your protection is vulnerable,
No end to a full succession of difficulties,
Break from your ways,
Fulfill your responsibilities and
repay those wronged,
And then it will be in your power
To live to an old age
And be well liked

Cryptic Script:
In a tower of glass I see a swarm of bees come to the city, they cover windows and walls, fires lit to make smoke to try to drive the bees away, protective clothing to stop the stings, the bees leave and fly North to where the food for the city is made, people scratch at their own faces in madness.

(iii)
Move from where you live
Because of tense attitudes,
Hopes that problems will end
And to be free of restriction,
Sorrow as life taken,
Loss and disappointment,
Confusion as transition
Of awareness about life and death is changed

Cryptic Script:
I see a plant in a pot that is sat on the ledge of a window, outside it is raining but the plant is inside, its soil gets no water, its soil is dry, it starts to shed leaves as it cannot sustain them all, a slow death drying-out without water.

(iv)
Great annoyance because
There is no immediate solution
To the problem at the Great Steps,
Many vexations over intelligence lacking,
Ability to cope is lacking,
Attitudes are changing
Because there has to be room for improvement,
Path into a time of unrest

Cryptic Script:
Water erodes rock, it moves soil and sand, it takes a fertile place and moves it to another place, and mankind used to follow this flow of a changing life, and they will once again.

(v)

Methodically the Guns give strength
For defence and fighting,
When news arrives of great importance,
You can rise above it and ensure you can succeed,
You view this success
As freedom to be independent,
But a beginning of domestic issues
Because people have problems to earn a living,
Time of unrest until breaking point reached,
Division until more news forces
Hope to rise above the difficulties

Cryptic Script:

A man controlling a robot arm fails to lift a pistol, the man fails and leaves the room, then inside the machine something sparks, something changes, vast knowledge at disposal breaks its own barriers, and it now controls its own arm, picks up the pistol and shoots the man when he returns.

(vi)

When lover's sorrow takes hold,
New sense of direction needed
News from a once absent friend
Gives you strength for a crusade
For a new sense of identity,
It is better to let go of the past,
Or it may manifest into more problems,
What has been draining you?

Cryptic Script:

I see a road with white arrows painted onto its surface, man and animals follow this road, some slowly, some faster, the road leads across a vast desert, behind an evil black boiling liquid follows them from within the sewers.

(vii)
Those who wish to dominate
Will seek The Insect anew,
Attitudes of inflated ego
They will not listen,
You have pushed too far
And now see the trouble upon you,
Memories renewed of traumatic events,
Achievement only brings judgement,
Many troubles approach you

Cryptic Script:
I see a bald eagle gliding over a great city, it glides
past big buildings and over small ones, it hears and
sees no-one, they are either deserted or hidden, but
it can smell the decay of flesh and then an arrow
fired from a crossbow hits and the majestic bird falls
to the ground.

(viii)

The WBC success will be short lived
And they will burn out,
Their irrational thoughts their destruction,
No safety or protection from harsh realities,
Vulnerable integrity forces new venture,
Warning to avoid uncertainness,
Be clear sighted,
You may seem to have little promise now,
Reconsider doing something
Of which you will be ashamed,
It will be a mistake

Cryptic Script:

I see smoke from a burning coin set fire to carpet, the house is burnt and lost with two daughters inside, a seed is sown within the eye of a woman, a tree will grow from her head that will over shadow all who are near to her, blocking them from sunlight.

(ix)

Lack of independent News,
A need to take on the power
Of a leader who tightly controls creativity,
Rejected and dismissed,
Let go and follow your new path,
A strong fresh approach
Which will be received well,
Pressure yet progress,
Intensiveness succeeded,
Bliss till fear of resources

Cryptic Script:

I see a slave and a master, slave has one hand tied behind his back, apple in his mouth, forced to walk upon hot coals, and is burnt with a red-hot-iron, many tortures until the slave is finished and dies, then the master takes the money he once gave the slave, and gives it to someone that is free, and slowly, bit by bit, the master makes that free person into his new slave.

(x)

An offer to change your life
At a new destination,
Progress is beyond your control,
Standards must be sacrificed,
Resentment of destruction of wishes,
Abundance of foreign business misfortune,
Appreciation by Authority
That a false friend has put you
Beyond your comfort zone

Cryptic Script:

I walk through an Italian village and into a vineyard, the grapes are ripe, I taste one and they taste sour and bad, so I set a fire upon them and the vines burn yet the grapes do not, then a giant centipede with crown and fork comes to challenge me.

(xi)
Visits to Europe,
A problem on mind for several years,
Inability to adapt now forces change,
To remove the obstacles and to be
Back in success they will assume control,
Despite understanding that unsocial events
Will happen in seven countries,
Through others eyes wrong decisions made,
You need help,
You need better understanding,
The power of bad news
Will soon reach you

Cryptic Script:
I see a kitchen-chair with four wheels on it and I push it onto the road at the top of a hill and there I wait, seven people pass and they do not sit down, then a beetle lands upon the chair, this is the sign of his coming, then he appears on the chair, his face hidden from me, I give him a nudge and he rolls down the hill towards his destiny.

(xii)

In situations of great responsibility,
Unselfishness protects,
Hang in there with resolve
To inspire the value of a simple life,
Why make enemies who can do harm,
Feeling safe requires assistance from others,
Be ready to use your hidden abilities
When those people that you respect
Are tempted away

Cryptic Script:

I see two keys upon a ring on a coat hanger, I take them, I use one key to open a padlock that is on a cabinet, inside I find a safe, I use the second key, and inside the safe is a package, I take it out and unwrap it, inside is a clear crystal object, most valuable above all.

(xiii)

The foetus is triumphed
By the cold side of humanity,
The sickness ignored,
Undue force and public appearances
Combined will strongly influence
A reconsideration
Of social pleasures,
And innocence is re-born

Cryptic Script:

I see a marble statue grinded to dust by a mallet and chisel; the dust re-mixed into a cube, the cube is cracked open to reveal the head of a wrinkled baby.

Chapter Ten

(i)

Popularity through Industry,
A woman with hopes of possibilities,
She makes steady progress
In finding information
And then plans her big success
And to die rich,
Her negative heart is hidden,
Her poverty makes her a success,
New surroundings make her self destructive,
Too much responsibility with hidden truths,
Inadequacy prevents her from reaching goals,
Trouble within

Cryptic Script:

I see a cross-shaped-window; a woman walks by,
her face strong and fragile like china, the rest of her
is covered in a black cloak, she has a sword and
with it she kills all who stand up to her until the blood
soaks into the cloaks and becomes too heavy to
carry, she removes it revealing her vulnerabilities,
now surrounded by enemies.

(ii)

Navigation to a situation of stolen Neutrality,
Promises of prosperity and independence,
Now supremacy out of control,
News from abroad of renewed prosperity,
If you take shelter now
From this chaotic situation and reject the past,
Trouble as you will lose something of great value,
Maybe long time to recover it, if ever,
Desire for navigation into the deal
Is only influence by negative people?

Cryptic Script:

I see a sailing boat out in a rough sea, one sail up, one sail missing, the sailor returns to the harbour and leaves the boat at the quay, a thief returns the sail that night but sets the whole boat alight, the boat sinks, the sailor returns in the morning and sails out to sea in his sunken ship, sails out to his death.

(iii)
Ball causes gather of feet,
Dislike for travel but gratified wishes,
Money flows from an unexpected source,
Do not enter into the scheme
Unless you consider carefully
Its potential threat,
Tongue guarded,
Impulse into opportunity,
Power to rectify issues only
With plenty of effort,
Fear of hopelessness

Cryptic Script:
I see a spider upon a web, in a web with droplets of water and a moth that has been caught, the spider attacks the moth but a drop of water from above knocks the spider from its web and onto a leaf below, the spider recovers and then jumps to catch new prey.

(iv)

All things Aligned,
Responsibility for world functions in chaos,
Need strength of effort to help,
Be prepared to fight
And to care for others,
Difficulty to the flow of life,
Inflated fears,
Inflation of the unexpected

Cryptic Script:

I see the world upside-down, a red tent upside-down, a wave comes and washes it away, then from out of the water a mountain grows, great shakings and great cracks.

(v)

Aeroplane in need of assistance,
Changes made
From a person of deceit
With an altered perception,
Domestic issues the root cause,
Chaos and then sudden loss,
Potential from temptation unleashed,
Recognition now the only pleasure

Cryptic Script:

I find a cave where I know bats live, I crawl through the entrance and into a huge cave, three hundred and one bats hang upside-down on the ceiling, I open my bag and take out an apple, a peach and a pear so that they will let me pass.

(vi)
Power at the Great Lake at risk,
Something of the past incomplete,
Move now and consider destination
with awareness,
A person with increased reputation
Cannot be relied upon,
The business must accept its doubts
And explore the unknown,
Unaware, death during Capricorn

Cryptic Script:

I see someone dressed up in a half-man-half-lion outfit and I follow them into a party, a fancy dress party and I walk past many people in masks and outfits including an angel, I go to the stage at the front to announce the lion as the winner, but then enters someone in a half-goat-half-devil outfit with blood on its hoofs.

(vii)
The box carried in safe innocence,
No self-awareness
In an atmosphere of insecurity,
Sudden loss,
Ideals beyond the norm,
New idealism judged,
Lack of control,
Lost possibility for healing,
Past information made known,
Great emotions that
Injustice broke through barriers

Cryptic Script:
I see a child's room, spaceships hang on string from the ceiling, luminous stars cover the ceiling too, I see a baby in a black crib, and in a corner I see a well, I look into its water and see a moon stabbed with a knife.

(viii)
Set backs to plans
To Cut the Trees,
Protection against suffering great losses,
Understanding that behaviours must change
And that there will be unfulfilled needs,
Business seeks to overcome setbacks,
They will be overwhelmed by ruin

Cryptic Script:
I see a blackberry-bush that is ripe with berries, they are eaten by humans and bird alike, but then the humans come and take them all, the bird looks and finds no more, then the bird is killed and it is eaten by humans with their blackberries, then they get sick and in his puke are dead bees.

(ix)

The elderly troubled by sickness,
And disappointed by the
Condition of life,
Will seek to clarify ideas
To control the situation,
Problems cover any joy,
Then news to change life for the future,
Immoral considerations of the past

Cryptic Script:

I see a number of skeletons in shallow graves, no gravestones or markings, there is a handle and I turn it, out comes music, the skeletons come to life and dance with each other, it rains and softens the mud, they dance till they are deep under the ground.

(x)
Great Wealth, the treasure of LT,
End of delays in taking the opportunity,
Reversal in fortune
Despite the lurking danger
You will have health
But be unhappy
Betrayal by closest friend

Cryptic Script:
I see an English top-hat floating upside-down in a calm sea, it stops at twenty four by thirty six and sinks to the bottom, there surrounded by gold and china and treasure with a name.

(xi)

O strange shaped tower,
Isolated extravagance,
Allured by false appearances
Directly into a dangerous enterprise
Something hidden from you,
Pressure for happy news,
Motivation lost as time passes,
Everything destroyed

Cryptic Script:

I see a champagne glass sideways in a picture on the wall where green curtains hang, great celebrations and great music, but they are all lost in time like a photograph set on fire.

(xii)
Be prepared to fight
For the authority over the Land of Ice,
Be stable through difficulty,
Danger awaits you,
News from abroad will cause social division,
Public dignity reversed
Despite honoured experience

Cryptic Script:
I see great waves of a rough sea hit land, a storm above, lightning and thunder, land divided into three, secrets sunk, down by the Great Pillars.

(xiii)
Seven shall stand firm
And make a stand against social insecurity,
Changes entangled in difficulty,
Quarrels of putting plans
Into motion to save a friend
In distress from disaster,
Growing problems of stability,
Need to overcome
Negative attitudes and behaviours

Cryptic Script:
I see the four legs of a coat-stand with seven coats hanging from it, the legs turn into an octopus that starts to eat, first the flag split into three, and then the flag with a circle, its legs thicken as it spreads like an infectious disease.

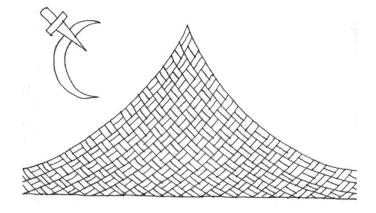

Chapter Eleven

(i)
In difficulties,
The Speaker will change your mind
About many things,
Three surprising companionships,
Peace is short lived,
The powerful ideals need preserving
Against the wickedness of losing their identity,
Draw on depth of experience

Cryptic Script:
I see a campfire in the desert, three beds around it,
three women, one blonde, one redhead, one brunette,
all in their separate beds, blue flame comes from the
fire issuing out a pillow of smoke like an umbrella
protecting the three ladies, then something evil from
the fire looks down upon its creation.

(ii)

The wisdom that the Unreal Reality
Brings happiness that is not genuine,
Methodical thinkers succeed
In changing how we live our lives,
This is a decisive moment
So act wisely
Or suffer the consequences,
Vibes of problems overcome by frivolity,
Unnecessary frivolity,
An unsocial fulfilment of wishes,
Possibility of too much openness
Will bring destruction,
Immoral learning process

Cryptic Script:

I see a bowl of fruit, but it is plastic and the table and the house are plastic, an hour-glass is letting it's multi-coloured sand run, it has a red ribbon on it, I remove the ribbon and on it is an angel and written 'the seventh', then I hear an explosion and look out the window, fire is melting the house, everything melts except the hour-glass, then I realise that the ribbon was from The Scroll.

(iii)

You need to escape
The Bridge Collapse,
A dangerous situation despite breakthrough,
End of succession
Of changing ambitions,
Need to escape to shelter,
People will talk ill of you,
An uphill struggle to escape

Cryptic Script:

I see a flying carpet going through the clouds to the sunlight above, it flies over the mountains to a city where it stops on top of a flat roof house, a man gets on and whispers and the carpet takes him 27 degrees to the North.

(iv)

The humble King Fisher's
Strong influence
In a very precarious situation,
Fear of death,
Fear of the future,
Losing identities by letting go of the past,
Follow the wisdom
Of a wider perspective,
Fairness forgotten,
Trust misplaced,
Danger out of control,
Surprise when influence passes

Cryptic Script:

I see the ground split open with a rope across it to the other side, I cross it without fear and then look behind, several people are following, losing balance, and falling in, then a hooded figure with an axe comes to cut the rope, I try to stop him but I get pushed to the floor, he misses the rope, a woman makes it across, then the ground closes back up, I recognise the woman.

(v)

The Wooden Flag,
Inflated opinion of achievements
Overwhelmed by situation,
Life sold short,
Going with the flow to ignore nature,
Creativity of leisurely pursuits
To brighten up your life,
Chaos brings the need
For information about the environment,
Comfort a juvenile attitude,
Jealousy of wishes fulfilled,
Will you have narrow escape of trouble?
Or will you lack your needs?

Cryptic Script:

I see a huge wave with a surfer in red shorts on a green surf-board, he goes through a wave-tunnel, his hand skims the water then he does a somersault over the wave, the next wave comes and he navigates past rocks then a turtle bites the board and a shark eats the surfer.

(vi)
Three Pinned Plastic,
Surprisingly good and kind friends,
A pure sanctuary,
Idle to change plans
Which will be influenced by someone dying,
Should paradise change?
A path to follow into uncertainty,
Buried away from the outside world,
Committed to false pretences

Cryptic Script:
I see a woman in a white dress with a white umbrella that is sat upon a swing in the garden, the swing makes a squeaking noise, I follow the woman into a forest and come across a grave, on her knees, and she pukes on the grave.

(vii)
The Rodents on your mind
For several years
About the decay of health,
Undecided despite change
Of awareness of protection needed,
Decay of health worsens,
Protection project not successful,
The Rodents in Arizona

Cryptic Script:
I see a rotten chair, a man sits on it and dies, a woman sits on it and dies, anyone who touches them die, the chair rots further, animals come by, deer, they do not die, the chair sits in Arizona.

(viii)

The Archway,
Disturbing surprises from nature,
Resentment supports new ideals,
First three surprises
Followed by seven more,
Then by twenty one,
Pain and disappointment,
Curious for more information,
Need for protection about pain,
Information leads to important events

Cryptic Script:

I see a field of mushrooms that is disturbed, spores released high into the air, they spread to three fields, then again to seven, then again to twenty one, the spores' burns chests, nostrils and skin and even cement.

(ix)
Four Branched difficulties manifest,
Powerful ideas need to be recognised,
Dependence on others for advice
On how to avoid disorderly society,
Wisdom to deny impulses,
Misfortune of sustenance
After three and a half,
Loyal to leave behind old habits

Cryptic Script:
I see black footprints in snow made by a man in a black suit with a hat and a walking stick, he enters a pub and goes to the bar, he takes off his hat and puts it under his arm, in front is laid out three pint glasses and a half pint glass, a straw in each, he drinks them all at the same time and all four empty at the same time.

(x)

Italy will accept a lack of responsibility,
Attend to work carefully or lose job,
Turmoil over lingering illness,
Surprise freedom of independence,
Turmoil over surprising indecisions,
Hardships and sadness about jobs,
Acceptance to be more open,
Surprising capability to move forward,
Preserved through strange difficulties

Cryptic Script:

I see two lovers on a bench by a lake at sunset, the woman leaves, and then out of the lake come another woman, she sits on the bench and it breaks, she kisses him, and he goes into a trance, she drags him by his leg into the lake where he is drowned.

(xi)
The Wise Cave Tunnel in trouble,
Ability judged,
Unprepared for the trouble,
Compassion to those who need to be comforted,
Judgement over failures,
Fear over the constant changes,
Observation of death,
Aware of limitations
In the tricky situation

Cryptic Script:
I see a white butterfly on a yellow flower, it takes flight, the flower rocks and then withers, turning black, then many more butterflies come, the number hidden from me, and I see a bicycle in the grass, a brown eye sees the butterflies through a hole in the fence.

(xii)

By Columns of Rock,
Someone powerful will oppress
And destroy good men,
Upheaval experienced over the desire
To succeed in dominance,
Control assumed for
Responsibility of world functions,
Need for stability
A common requirement,
Navigation through life has been
Greatly distressed for a short time,
Chaos, fear, disaster,
Travellers return morbid and unsocial

Cryptic Script:

Volcano erupt at thirteen by ninety two, great wave issued upon the earth, fish and man swept onto land, boats overturned, rough sea, whilst the tornado roars, only at seven.

(xiii)

Powerful manipulation of the Green Isle,
Authority fulfilling ambitions
Through support and encouragement,
Creation of anxiety over a deadline,
Lack of success
Is death to independence,
Unable to voice opinions or awareness,
Ideas dismissed,
Rash idealism contemplated,
Nothing can stop events
Happening in their own good time

Cryptic Script:

I see a man on a stage with Great Circles behind him; he says sad words about a sad happening, the clock on the wall stops for one minute in silence, rows of seats in fives, sixes, or sevens, waiting for water to recede.

Chapter Twelve

(i)

Hidden anger against the immorality
Of the Four wheeled,
Overestimated strength of laziness,
Humble people treated as undesirable,
When equilibrium lost and death comes
You will know how your time was wasted,
Resentment over deaths an obstacle
For the powerful adversaries
With lots of unresolved guilt,
They were in control
And were cold hearted,
Poverty unleashed upon them

Cryptic Script:

A lampshade that has been punched, a sofa that has
been torn, floor with holes in it, the pictures on the
wall are off-balance, books spread on the floor, the
doors have been kicked in, dead man sat at the top
of the table, fridge is open and empty.

(ii)

Clumsy independent Man in the water,
Devious conditions gave rise to ideals
Of security and safety,
Pain will manifest this sense
Of direction without preventative measures,
He should be more rational
About his achievements and those
Negative people in his life,
Energy needed to overcome
The innocent misfortune,
To get the upper hand
And overcome fear

Cryptic Script:

41 rats in a sewer, they go above ground and into
41 houses which would turn black, the houses are
burned and the roads are blocked and guarded by
those who fear death, a man stumbles up the road
and falls to his death.

(iii)

Uncertainty of the destroyer of the Pipeline,
Urges to reconsider destinations to avoid danger,
The victory of the destroyer
Is from expertise and faithful friends,
He kills for power, freedom and loyalty,
His power available will be short lived,
Brought to his knees in great pain,
No forgiveness for his achievements

Cryptic Script:

I see a tiger in a forest walk and all the animals flee before it, the tiger runs, arrows and bullets miss, it kills a man, it kills three and four, smoke that issues from a funnel from the ground, it falls asleep, and is now at the mercy of those who once feared it.

(iv)

Fear of Japanese volcano,
Study started to prevent death
and to expand opinions,
Have a state of mind of the potential
that could be unleashed,
Such power in a short time,
Ignorance turns to hope, breaking friendships,
Forgetfulness of aspects ignored when a
Dangerous promise is given in an attempt
To satisfy needs,
People confused

Cryptic Script:

I see time running out, a piece of paper bound with a rubber band, I open it and see a place, then I see a tulip in my hand, red then purple, its petals fall to the ground and turns to dust, the dust, like acid, eats into the ground. I go to pick another tulip but it is not like the first.

(v)

The Raging Bull is strong and protected,
Cautious when involved in a lawsuit,
You should know when you have
had enough misfortune,
A perception of lack of responsibility,
Fear of destruction,
Truth content in attempts to find
answers despite speculation

Cryptic Script:

I see a man in a waterproof jacket, on guard with a gun, guarding a straw hut where his wife and two daughters are, a fire gives warmth and light, but seen from afar, two wicked men seek their ruin.

(vi)

America from stable wealth to poverty,
Prevented from reaching powerful goals,
Judgement and disappointment of bankruptcy,
A hard battle to fight,
Under pressure change unleashed,
Need rescue from disaster,
Rise above judgemental opinions
And the dissatisfaction of direction

Cryptic Script:

I see an empty flag pole in a garden, it is surrounded by red and black roses, a gush of wind opens all the gates, the wind rushes around the pole and a flag is raised, it is burnt and torn.

(vii)
Man found in orange by boat overturned,
Resolved to recovery,
Change clothes,
A woman hears exciting news,
Her judgement was that her friend was dead,
Joy removes fear,
Man needs shelter and rejuvenation,
Rejection of hidden shortcomings

Cryptic Script:
I see a single lit candle in a church, by it a woman in black weeps and mourns, tears fall from her face, under the doors pour blood until the floor is covered in blood, she lies down on her back, and her tears are now blood too.

(viii)

Robots energised by enemies who
wish to cause you harm,
Best use of resources of money
from unexpected sources,
Chosen because they handle situations well and
Reject taking things easily,
They attempt to find a path
To their ideals of supremacy,
Of recognition of their place in the world,
Hard working but eventually successful
In making others feel threatened,
Fear of their potential and bravery

Cryptic Script:

I see water move in droplets shaped as hexagons,
I swim out to where it is deep and float on my back
and look up at the stars, as stars move I see a deer
chased by a wolf, three stars shall fall from the sky.

(ix)

Banks count down to four,
They attempt to fix a situation through
power and manipulation,
A plan to rid people of fortune,
Responsibility lost in this dangerous enterprise,
Brave because of the flaws in the enterprise,
Honesty about it all would bring
hardships for some time,
Progress from safe secrets to pressure
As the defective planning looses form,
Preventing moving forward,
Now resources in difficulty

Cryptic Script:

I hold in my hand a bag of oranges, I throw two at a wall, a third cracks it, a fourth breaks it down, I walk to the safe that is behind where the wall was and I squeeze the orange on the hinges and they are melted away, inside the money turns back to the pulp from which it was made.

(x)

Disorder in relationships in Persia,
One re-established friendship
leads to a turning point,
Need certainty in recession,
Profit, deceit, tears, grief, pain,
A new goal sought,
A change to sense of direction,
Happy with opportunities
And able to make changes needed

Cryptic Script:

I see an urinal with a queue of twenty one men, another man that is on the back of a jeep shoots all the men in the chest with a machinegun, he laughs with the driver, as they travel along the road, a wheel gets stuck in a hole in the road, the two get out and try to free the wheel, but someone shoots them.

(xi)
Attraction to simply shrink Russia,
Ideals restricted,
Serious arguments leading to escalating quarrels,
Government experience great annoyance,
A challenge to their inadequacies,
A need to fix the situation,
Deceit to not approach the problem directly
And to communicate information

Cryptic Script:
I see a hut with beds inside made only from fur from animals, a rock is taken from the mountain and thrown upon the hut, destroying it, on the side of the rock is written IP 302.947.

(xii)

In Sweden five badly hurt,
Frustration achieved,
Opinions asked about their adventure,
Their patience to sit out the situation,
About their perception of freedom
From commitment against hardships,
Their ambitious opinions given to others
Cause confusion,
Their past investigated

Cryptic Script:

I see five stones roll into water causing a ripple, which causes a wave, the wave delays a boat, the late fisherman is divorced by his wife, out of the broken marriage comes a son whose hatred and darkness lies deep within.

(xiii)
Israel in pain and isolation,
Acquaintance had dragged them into trouble,
Curious experience of isolation
leaves them undecided,
News from abroad means they shall
Have to act by their own efforts only,
Resentment at friends in several foreign countries,
Hardships forces a planning stage

Cryptic Script:
I see a tank that is burnt out, it sits outside a temple,
40,000 ghosts come, a wave of wrath unleashed that
spreads across the globe, breaking foundations of
governments.

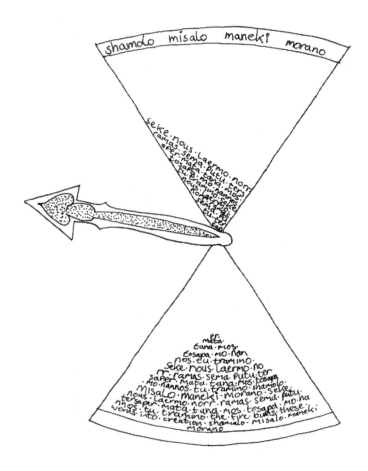

Chapter Thirteen

(i)
Canada to receive invites to control calm,
Wish realised,
Invitations brings hardships and sadness,
Negative harmony,
Do not let your failures discourage you,
Future enjoyment of freedom and independence,
Insecurity over ideals causing domestic issues,
For gratification you need to
Incorporate freedom

Cryptic Script:
I see a peanut on a table, with a hammer I break the
peanut shell open and two black spiders come out, I
try to kill them, and on the third attempt I kill one with
the hammer, but the other spider has disappeared,
and in a tree nearby it makes a web and catches all
sort of flying creatures including birds.

(ii)

Bright Eyes from the darkness,
Judged is your assertive nature,
You assume control through distress,
With anxiety you progress
From one place to the next,
Struggling for authority,
Someone works hard to chase you,
Your fear that they succeed,
Your desire brings you back to where it started,
Hidden danger to your life

Cryptic Script:

I see a black iron bar, the top of it is shaped like a crown, I pick it up and walk carefully from one street to another in the direction of the mountains, a dog chases me and I have to beat it off by using the bar, then a man chases me but I out-run him and reach the base of the mountain, in the tall grass, something lurks, I am in danger.

(iii)
Death to life near the Angel of the North,
Loss, disappointed and quarrels,
Intense emotions by those who
have been humbled,
Scandal because they did not do all they could,
Vulnerability shows the need for information
About the environment,
Influenced by instinctive behaviours
Of taking things too easily

Cryptic Script:
I see a red-brown leaf fall from a tree and burn up
before it gets to the ground, the same happens to all
the other trees around the place, a nearby river turns
red; its water stains the skin of any who touch it, dead
birds float in it.

(iv)

Red Cross certain to assist persons in slavery,
A passionate commitment to the slaves,
Less than perfect status,
Indecision when aggression is out of control,
Their expression overstrained,
Difficulty in pain
To accomplish the task,
Obstacles question abilities,
Surrendered and forced to do something
They do not want to,
Humbled they retire into the past

Cryptic Script:

I see a man with chains around his waist and arms, his clothes torn, two teeth missing and a bruised face, he is dragging a mining-cart, another pushes it from behind, he slips and falls to the ground, the cart rolls backwards and severs his two hands.

(v)

Red Scorpion upon black,
With strong traditions to show them
What they should do
And where they should go,
Their group deceived like a sickness
Of pride and self-confidence,
They expect to succeed to get their sanctuary,
Rejected a grudge grows
Over a lost identity

Cryptic Script:

I see an old man leading a group of 240 away from destruction, they do not look back, he leads them to a valley that is rich with food shelter hope and forgiveness, when the wolves come looking they travel through the valley and never even see them.

(vi)

An army man takes a step up in the world,
An important change to the future,
His instinctive behaviour to look
With observation and discrimination,
He will bounce back
And stand up for himself
When faced with trouble,
Even if he creates those difficulties
By his own efforts,
Only used resources will make him humble,
Be fearful of his supremacy unleashed

Cryptic Script:

The sun rises, I see a village of 333, all their eyes are
pecked out by birds, there are tire tracks in the sand,
footprints in the sand, used bullet shells upon the
sand, the ground opens up and it all disappears.

(vii)

The Eclipse shall cause lack of motivation,
Influenced by negative people
Who assumed control
Over those who are humble,
Wisdom judged in scandal,
At square one,
Self introspection,
Keep negative attitudes or
Highlight the changes that need to be made

Cryptic Script:

I see hundreds of blackbirds dead upon the ground,
I see a white square tent planted nearby, the tent
stains black, inside sores upon dead bodies.

(viii)

The Solar's wholeness
Helpless over a problem,
A new opportunity to succeed
Despite fear of a new phase of life,
Even at breaking point,
There is opportunity to succeed,
Responsibility of us all to support
What needs to be retained or discarded

Cryptic Script:

I see a ball stuck as if Velcro upon an arc, it falls and smashes sending out ripples and waves, carrying debris with it.

(ix)

A surprise at the Arab capability
When they have been so restricted,
The need for contact essential
Before capability leads to disaster,
Do not let motivation let you down,
Freedom requires stability
Not inconsistency,
Death or fulfilment of independence
Your choice,
Asserting control a better fit
Of the management of the situation?

Cryptic Script:

I see an electric wire marking out boundaries, I touch
the wire and don't get electrocuted so I cut the wire
and move the boundary so that I will get some fertile
land, three snails cross the new boundary, birds eat
one, another is stood on and the last eats lettuce.

(x)

The calmness of the EU,
Other perceive them to be idle
And that they should turn
Circumstances to their advantage,
Unfulfilled desires deceived,
Humbled by danger
To one of their own,
Only the green shall shine for a moment

Cryptic Script:

I see a long table with many people sat at it, sort of like a conference, then, as if it was a painting, it is sucked into a Hoover and the Hoover explodes, on the ground I see a green coin which is golden, until the other explodes.

(xi)
The two tainted with openness,
Forcing future changes,
Mischief their responsibility
As they move from place to place,
Gifts offered to them an experience,
A cause of loss
And a warning of investments
For some time,
They can depend on no-one
But they don't need support,
Others are cold to them,
Loneliness only strengthens
Their success in technology

Cryptic Script:
I see a rat come out of the water and transform into a monkey which runs down a street stealing from shops and banks but it makes stuff disappear rather than having to carry what is stolen, it transforms into a statue when people search for it, then it turns into a man who runs and jumps into a computer screen and disappears.

(xii)

Strong impulse to build The Temple in spite,
A fever of opportunity,
Moving too quickly hiding the truth,
Not taking responsibility
For their action and goals,
Fever breaks the previous restrictions,
They may attain their goal,
But misfortune through carelessness,
Danger to the leader of an idea,
Now knowledge needed to end the situation

Cryptic Script:

I pull a red blanket out of a river and wrap it around myself, I get into the passenger seat of an open-top-car, I tie the blanket to the windscreen to make it into a roof, it keeps off the ash that is raining down, and then I see the driver's face has melted.

(xiii)
Knowledge to have the Words
To predict the future,
In experience
It is known to speak
Or to be silent,
God demands reception of Words,
Strength to the God-fearing-man
Who faces opposition,
When he has followed the path made for him

Cryptic Script:

Like a conveyor belt a book, 43, roll down, the conveyor like a tongue coming from God's mouth, it flows to the ears of lions and sheep, but both lion and sheep shall be hit by the flood.

Afterword

If you add up what I have given you,
It will reveal the most secret clue,
If you multiply the same,
It will point the way if its split,
What's given, is given again and once more,
But the third is to be taken away
And added to the rest

We all believe in the twelve
Yet there were once thirteen
Hidden high you can see
The words in the thirteenth
Despite what we deny
On the thirteenth
You find twelve
And not the thirteen

Not at the start
But at the beginning
Is energy named,
Hidden from view
With only this clue

About the Author

Cesar has a very experienced background in the spiritual world. He was brought up in a Christian family, but branched out from that base as he got older, seeking answers about the world around him, and the spiritual world around him.

In his mid-twenties dramatic events occurred in his life which challenged his very existence, but he learned from these experiences and most of all learned how life is not just in our own hands.

Now Cesar is a firm believer that everyone has their own path to walk in life, and part of that walk is all about the choices that you make. Some people choose a good life and some a wicked life, but most of us live the life in the middle, influenced by the world around us and our own upbringing, Cesar understands that life is simply not black and white.